DOGS

BY M. C. SWENSEN

PUBLISHED BY THE CHILD'S WORLD®

Published by The Child's World®
1980 Lookout Drive • Mankato, MN 56003-1705
800-599-READ • www.childsworld.com

For Schotzie, Pippa, and Max.

ACKNOWLEDGMENTS
The Child's World®: Mary Swensen, Publishing Director
The Design Lab: Design
Michael Miller: Editing
Sarah M. Miller: Editing

DESIGN ELEMENTS
© Doremi/Shutterstock.com

PHOTO CREDITS
© alexei_tm/Shutterstock.com: 12-13; Annette Shaff/Shutterstock.
com: 11; Hannamariah/Shutterstock.com: 16; ivkatefoto/
Shutterstock.com: 19; Jagodka/Shutterstock.com: 6-7; Matthew
Williams-Ellis/Shutterstock.com: 20-21; Mikkel Bigandt/Shutterstock.
com: cover; Rita Kochmarjova/Shutterstock.com: 10, 15; vit-plus/
Shutterstock.com: 5; Vivienstock/Dreamstime.com: 8-9

ISBN: 9781503808263
LCCN: 2015958482

Printed in the United States of America
Mankato, MN
June, 2016
PA02308

Table of Contents

Cute Dogs

"Woof!" What is that dog saying? Dogs can be big or small. They have four legs and two ears. Some have a long tail. Others have a short tail.

DID YOU KNOW?

DOGS CAN WEIGH ANYWHERE BETWEEN 3 AND 175 POUNDS (1 AND 79 KILOGRAMS).

DID YOU KNOW?

DOGS CANNOT SWEAT. THEY MUST PANT TO KEEP COOL.

Furry Coats

Dogs are covered in soft fur. This fur is called a **coat**. A dog's coat can be curly or straight. It can be short or long. Some dogs have a very long coat!

Many Colors

Dogs can be many colors.
Many dogs are brown,
black, or white. Some
dogs are just one color.
Other dogs have spots
or patches.

DID YOU KNOW?

DOGS HEAR TEN TIMES BETTER THAN PEOPLE.

DID YOU KNOW?

THERE ARE ABOUT 400 MILLION DOGS IN THE WORLD.

Playing

Dogs have a lot of energy.
They like to run and play.

Some dogs like to swim. They
paddle with their feet.

DID YOU KNOW?

WOLVES AND DOGS ARE ANIMAL RELATIVES.

Toys

Many dogs like to play with toys. Balls and sticks are fun for dogs. Dogs also like to chew on things.

Baby Dogs

Baby dogs are called **puppies**. They cannot see when they are born. They do not open their eyes until they are nine days old. Puppies drink milk from their mother.

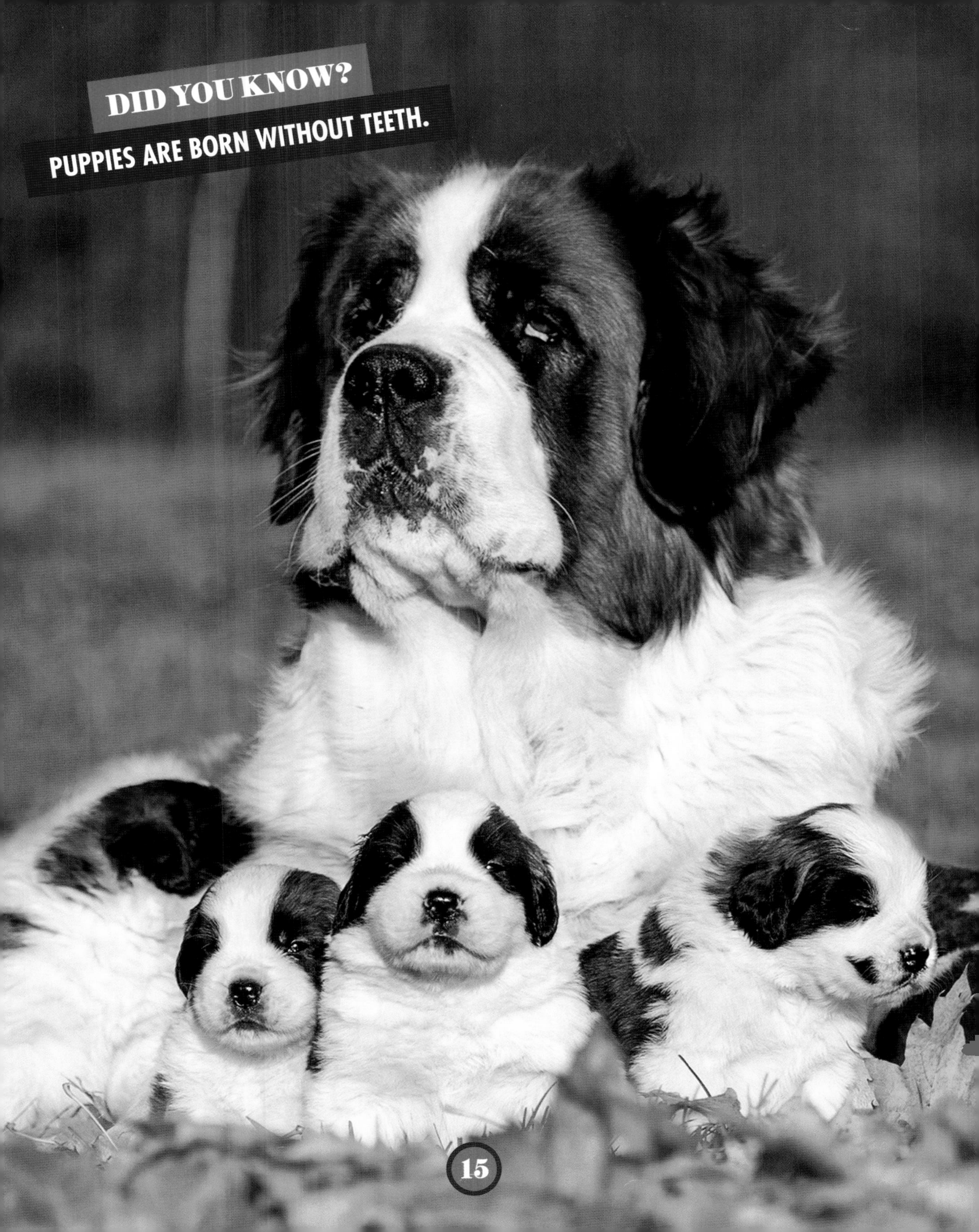

DID YOU KNOW?

PUPPIES ARE BORN WITHOUT TEETH.

Eating

Adult dogs eat meat foods. Pet dogs eat dog food from a store. It has meat flavors. The food can be wet or dry. Dogs also like fresh water to drink.

Great Pets

Dogs are great pets. They can live everywhere. Dogs live in houses and apartments. Dogs live on farms, too.

Dogs are smart and gentle. They like to play and run. They make great pets. Would you like a pet dog?

DID YOU KNOW?

DOGS ARE VERY SMART. THEY CAN BE TRAINED TO HELP PEOPLE.

Glossary

COAT (KOHT) A coat is a dog's covering of fur.

PADDLE (PAD-dul) To paddle is to make short movements with the arms (or legs for dogs).

PANT (PANT) To pant is to breathe in short, quick puffs.

PUPPIES (PUP-peez) Puppies are baby dogs.

RELATIVES (REL-uh-tivs) Relatives are people or animals that come from the same family.

To Learn More

IN THE LIBRARY

Baines, Becky. *National Geographic Kids Everything Dogs: All the Canine Facts, Photos, and Fun You Can Get Your Paws On!* Washington, DC: National Geographic Society, 2012.

Clutton-Brock, Juliet. *DK Eyewitness Books: Dog.* New York, NY: DK Publishing, 2014.

Crisp, Marty. *Everything Dog: What Kids Really Want to Know about Dogs.* Chanhassen, MN: NorthWord Press, 2003.

ON THE WEB

Visit our Web site for links about dogs:
childsworld.com/links

Note to Parents, Teachers, and Librarians: We routinely verify our Web links to make sure they are safe and active sites. So encourage your readers to check them out!

Index

ABOUT THE AUTHOR

M. C. Swensen has lived in Minnesota all her life. When she's not reading or writing, M. C. enjoys spending time with her husband and dogs and traveling to interesting places.